Wilderness Album Series
DINOSAURS
Nature stories for children

Author
Dr. George E. Lammers
Curator of Geology
Manitoba Museum of Man & Nature

Illustrations
Betsy Thorsteinson

This book is dedicated to my family.

All conversions from metric to imperial are averaged.

A Sterling/Hyperion book
© 1990 Hyperion Press Limited
All rights reserved.

Sterling Publishing Co., Inc.
387 Park Avenue South,
New York, NY 10016

Produced by Hyperion Press Limited
300 Wales Avenue, Winnipeg, MB
Canada R2M 2S9

ISBN: 0-920534-47-3

Distributed in Canada by Sterling Publishing
c/o Canadian Manda Group
P.O. Box 920, Station U, Toronto, Ontario
Canada M8Z 5P9

Printed in U.S.A.

The Wilderness Album Series includes nature stories for children plus scientific information and line drawings. Titles in the series include *Vanishing Animals, Extinct Animals, Tropical Birds, Venomous Animals, Animals of the Dark, Animal Invaders, Small Mammals, Large Mammals* Vols. I and II, *Birds* Vols. I and II, *Owls in North America, Insects, Butterflies & Moths, Fish, Time & Life* (Fossils), *Dinosaurs, Wildflowers, Trees, Wild Edibles, Invertebrates, Reptiles & Amphibians.*

CONTENTS

Christine and Jacob Go To The Museum

It was Saturday and Christine and Jacob wondered what they could do.

"I know," said Mother. "Let's go to the museum."

"That's a good idea," said Dad. "Afterwards, I'll treat you all to lunch."

Christine's and Jacob's uncle worked at the museum and arranged to meet them there, in the laboratory where he worked. He was interested in learning from fossil bones that he dug from the earth. People called him a paleontologist. He had been on several expeditions collecting fossilized bones of dinosaur skeletons and had helped assemble them into a large exhibit at the museum. In the summer, he promised to take Christine and Jacob with him to the Red Deer River area in Alberta, Canada, which is one of the most important dinosaur "bone beds" in the world. He had some research to do there, and wanted the children to learn more about his work and dinosaurs.

"Hi, kids," Uncle Ned greeted them. "C'mon back to my lab. I've got some new pictures of fossils to show you. A friend of mine is working in the Gobi desert in Mongolia and he sent them. It's a site as good as the Alberta one. He found some well-preserved dinosaur tracks and the remains of plants and other animals that lived alongside dinosaurs."

"But that was millions of years ago," Christine said. "How could the tracks last all this time?"

"Two hundred and twenty-five million to be exact!" Uncle Ned replied. "When the animals died, their skeletons were eventually covered with earth. Minerals in the groundwater that flows beneath the earth's surface preserved the bones. After a long time, as the earth moved and eroded, the hardened bones were slowly exposed at the surface. The tracks were preserved by sand and clay being washed into them. When this later eroded, it revealed the tracks. In North America, sometimes parts of a skeleton and tracks are found by ranchers when they're working on the range."

Jacob laughed. "Think how excited Grandpa would be if that happened during branding!"

"That's true," Uncle Ned laughed too. "And Grandpa wouldn't be the only one. But that would be nothing like the excitement caused by the first dinosaur discovery! In 1841, an English doctor and his wife were out walking near their country home in Sussex. Imagine their surprise when they found the bones of a huge skeleton. No one had ever seen a creature like that before. The scientists who came to see it called it *Iguanodon* or "iguana tooth" because its teeth looked like lizard's teeth. The skeleton looked ferocious, and scientists borrowed the Greek words deinos (terrible) and sauros (reptiles) to give the skeleton a name. That's why we call them dinosaurs. The one in Sussex was the first dinosaur skeleton. But soon after that scientists began to look for more remains and they found them in North and South America, Asia, Africa, Australia, and recently, in Antarctica.

"Well," said Christine, "those dinosaurs certainly got around."

"Right," replied Uncle Ned. "They lived before the continents separated completely, so at times there was one big land mass where they could roam freely. When the continents did begin to separate, there were land bridges such as the Bering Strait for them to cross from continent to continent."

Iguanodon

Its discovery in England in the early 1800s marks the first dinosaur to be collected in a scientific manner. Many of the same genus were later found in the coal fields of Belgium in the late 1800s. Notice the large spikes on the front limbs. At first, these were thought to be horns that belonged on the head until they were found attached to the hands in later specimens. *Iguanodon* was a very efficient herbivore with teeth specialized for this purpose. The toes were quite hoof-like.

Uncle Ned Finds Clues In Rocks

"Did dinosaurs live in a jungle?" Christine asked. "Was the temperature like it is today?"

"Did they live in one place all their lives?" Jason said.

Uncle Ned laughed at all the questions. "It's difficult for us to know how dinosaurs lived. They existed for one hundred forty million years and then they suddenly disappeared. It's one of the big mysteries of animal investigations."

"Look at this, Uncle Ned," called Christine from the workbench. She was holding up a piece of fossil in a rock. "It looks like a leaf was stuck in here."

"You're right, Christine. I have a lot of these rocks and that's how I get clues about how dinosaurs lived and what the climate was like then and what other animals were around. For instance, we know that dinosaurs were vertebrates similar to fish, amphibians, birds, and mammals because they have vertebrae that form a backbone. Because of characteristics of the skull, dinosaurs are reptiles, one of the major groups of reptiles."

"Why are there so many different kinds of dinosaurs?" said Christine as she looked at the pictures in some of the books on her uncle's desk.

"There are many different species," Uncle Ned told her. "Basically they all have dinosaur characteristics but over the years some changes took place. When dinosaurs first appeared, the climate of the world was warm and dry and this weather controlled the vegetation that could exist. Cycads and ferns grew by the rivers and seaways and conifers grew on the highlands. These were part of the dinosaurs' diet. Later, when the climate cooled slightly, more modern deciduous trees appeared, you know, the ones that lose their leaves in autumn. Dinosaurs ate these leaves in the spring and summer, but they would have had to look for other food in the fall when the leaves had dropped. They might have had to travel to find something to eat, so some dinosaurs adapted to eat meat as well. Eating other food, adapting to changing temperatures, traveling great distances, even having to fight over dwindling food supplies made a difference in how they looked and behaved. This caused the variety of dinosaurs you see in the book."

"I bet they could have grown horns or longer claws or had to develop more muscles in their legs or become a different color," said Jacob.

"Exactly," said Uncle Ned. "Soon some of them looked quite different and we've given them different names. Some of the differences were due to the age of the animal or its sex, just as we see differences among people. Dinosaurs did develop horns. Some had different types of body ornamentation or the proportions of their bodies were different. Some walked on two legs and some walked on four legs."

The children were fascinated and they pressed Uncle Ned for more information.

"This great variety expresses the way they made their living — as grazers on grass and shrubs or browsers on trees or eaters of flesh or insect eaters, and so on. By their similarities or differences, the paleontologist determines how much they are related. This contributes to our understanding of the dinosaurs and answers some of your questions, Jacob."

Acrocanthosaurus and *Pleurocoelus*

Trackways provide scientists with information about walking or running behavior. It is through the study of trackways that "herding" was noted amongst sauropods and the stalking of prey by carnivorous dinosaurs. Trackways are a snapshot of the past — a moment in time. This scene took place along a coastal mud flat in Texas. Notice the long vertebral spines on the *Acrocanthosaurus* suggesting a fin from the neck down the tail.

Could We Have Lived When Dinosaurs Lived?

Jacob was curious about the environment on earth during the time of dinosaurs. "If dinosaurs first appeared during the Triassic, what other animals were around then?"

"Well," said Uncle Ned, "there certainly were many insects, as well as different kinds of fish, lizards, amphibians, and mammals. There was an inland sea and many rivers, so dinosaurs would have been close to water and all the vegetation that grew nearby such as ferns, seed ferns, cycads, and scouring rushes. A great variety of conifers grew at higher elevations and these were also food for the dinosaurs. There were lots of trees and shrubs but no flowering plants."

"They must have eaten a lot to fill such a large stomach," said Christine.

"That's true, but remember, the larger ones were probably less active than the larger mammals that live today, so they may have needed less food," said Uncle Ned.

There were very few bigger enemies to prey upon these large vegetable eaters, so they could lead a leisurely existence and eat whenever they wanted to," Christine's father said. He and Mother had come into the workshop and were looking at Uncle Ned's fossils.

"The warm climate remained for millions of years," Uncle Ned continued, "so I expect that dinosaurs lived easily. But when the Jurassic period began, the weather became more seasonal and there were severe droughts and water was sometimes in short supply. This meant that dinosaurs would have had to wander farther in search of food and drink. After several million years, however, when the Cretaceous began, the weather was more diversified. There were flowering plants and modern coniferous trees that replaced the primitive conifers and cycads. The flowering plants allowed the further development of pollinating insects, birds, and mammals."

"Such a great change in the environment must have made a change in the dinosaurs' lives," Mother observed.

"I'll bet," said Christine. "And if mammals were starting to develop, that means that people will evolve after that. Isn't that true, Uncle Ned?"

"In fact, it was the beginning of the end for dinosaurs," Uncle Ned said. "Mammals were barely beginning to compete with dinosaurs and by the time of the dinosaurs' extinction, mammals were well on their way to becoming the dominant vertebrates on land. Of course, it wasn't until sixty some million years later that man was to enter the scene."

"I'm sure dinosaurs fought each other and probably killed each other, too," said Jacob. "I'll bet some of the mammals even hunted dinosaurs' eggs and ate them. I'm beginning to feel sorry for dinosaurs."

"I don't think we should feel sorry for dinosaurs," said Uncle Ned. "You see, they had lived for a very long time — about one hundred and forty million years. While they may have felt pressure from the mammals, they were here much longer than man has been on the earth. But we know they did move about to accommodate their way of life. When the continents were joined together, the fossils we find of dinosaurs indicate that the same types were found in several places. That means they roamed freely. Later, when the continents were placed more or less how they appear today, different kinds of dinosaurs appeared in different land areas. They adapted to the areas and were not able to cross the oceans to other places."

"If we could look for fossils under the Antarctic ice or in the Brazilian jungle, we might get a lot more clues about what kind of dinosaurs lived where," Christine said.

"Listen, Christine," Jacob said, "there's no way anyone can get those bones. We'd better concentrate on what we can find."

"Well," Uncle Ned told them, "the very earliest dinosaurs are being collected from northwestern Argentina. So you see they did travel at one time. This new find is providing new information we haven't known before."

Baryonyx

Baryonyx means heavy claw. The claws are so distinctive on this animal that it has been nicknamed "claw." Because the claws and associated fish were fossilized together, scientists suggest that the fish might have been slapped from the water in the same way that modern bears catch fish. This dinosaur was first discovered in 1986 in England by an amateur fossil hunter. Maybe someday you will find a new dinosaur! Notice the head is similar to a crocodile. *Baryonyx* had twice as many teeth as similar theropods of the time.

Dinosaur Anatomy

"You might think that dinosaurs were big and clumsy creatures," continued Uncle Ned, "but they were pretty streamlined for their time. They evolved from creatures called archeosaurs and the one big difference was the way that dinosaurs could walk and run. In fact, dinosaurs' legs were under their bodies. Creatures before them, even though they were similar in size, had legs spreading out to the sides of their bodies — like lizards."

"Wow!" said Jacob. "Imagine having legs out to the side and trying to move a big heavy body around."

"Well you couldn't go very fast," said Uncle Ned, "and that's probably why the dinosaur was able to get the food easier and travel long distances. The dinosaurs had a better way to survive and this gave them an advantage over the other creatures."

"Having legs and feet would help dinosaurs move about," said Chrstine, "but what did they use for defense? Did they just run away when another dinosaur chased them?"

"No, I don't think so," said Jacob. "Look at these pictures, Christine. And look at this one. It's got front feet with a bladed claw that looks like a scythe. I'll bet it could cut and slash its way through anything. That one with the big horns would have to stand and fight. I don't think he could walk very fast on those kind of feet."

"You're right, Jacob," said Uncle Ned. "Dinosaurs adapted to their surroundings so they could defend themselves and find food. I think some of them had armored skin so it would take some pretty big teeth to bite through it.

"This one has a long spiked tail," said Jacob. "One swish and you'd be a goner. Some of them seemed to have spines to protect them and others look like they could fight back."

"Yes," pointed out Mother, "and this one has a sharp horn that could be very intimidating. I wonder if the spikes on this one's head protected him from injury or if the spikes were only some kind of ornamentation."

"That reminds me, Uncle Ned," Christine said. "Did dinosaurs have large brains? Were they intelligent animals?"

"All our evidence suggests they were intelligent and as competitive as the mammals and birds of the time. The predators would need to be sharp to ambush the others for food. The fact that groups of animals like dinosaurs lasted so long through time would require intelligence to survive and adapt."

Tenontosaurus and *Deinonychus*
The *Tenontosaurus* is being attacked by an agile, wolf-like pack of *Deinonychus* (which means terrible claw). The larger herbivorous dinosaur could only lash its massive tail in defense. This would have little effect on the aggressive carnivores' sharp claws and teeth. It is interesting that four such skeletons were actually found fossilized together, suggesting that the scene depicted here could have happened. *Deinonychus* probably killed its prey by disemboweling it.

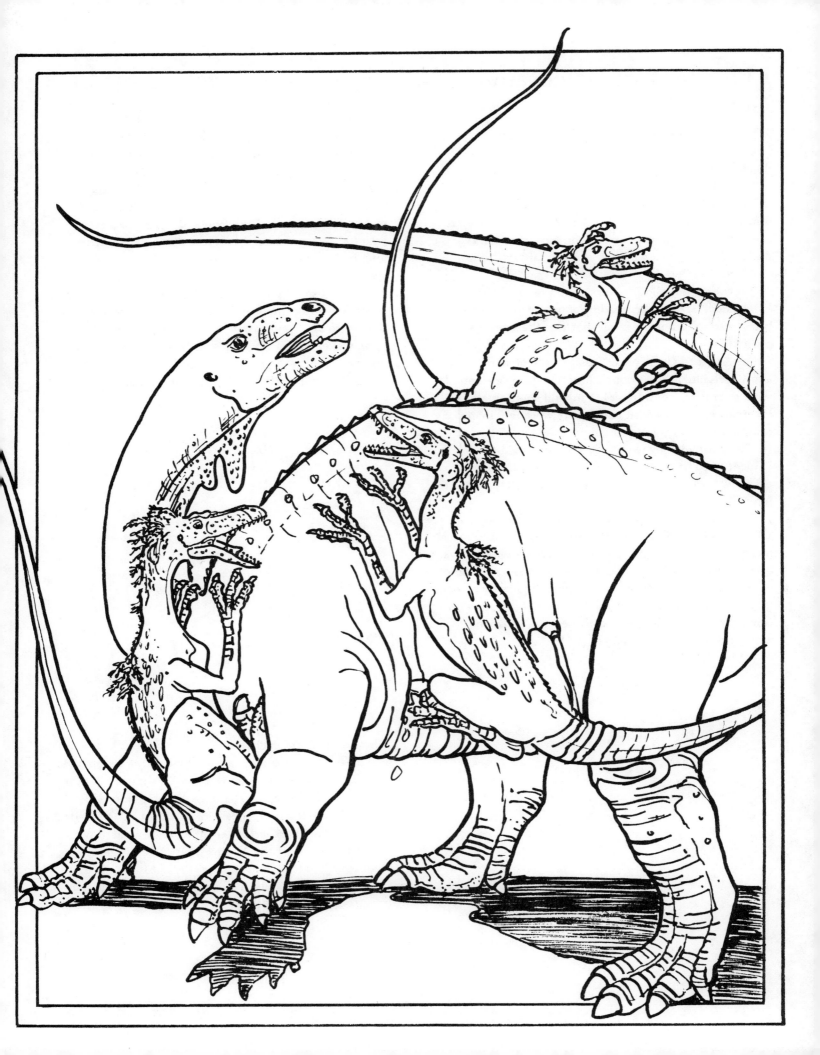

I Wonder How Dinosaurs Got So Big?

"These dinosaurs look like monsters." Christine was looking through Uncle Ned's books. "How come we don't have such huge animals today?"

"Actually, we do. The present day blue whale is the largest known animal to have existed and the largest dinosaurs probably weighed a little less. But dinosaurs are certainly the largest animals to have ever walked on land." Uncle Ned was enjoying his talk with the children.

"Of course not all dinosaurs were the same size," Father said. "I remember reading about a baby herbivorous (grass-eating) dinosaur fossil that was the size of a pigeon!"

"Yes," agreed Uncle Ned, "fossil skulls of some fully adult individuals from South America that were found were only three centimeters (1 in) and some small carnivorous (meat-eating) dinosaurs were less than sixty centimeters (24 in) in total length."

"Don't forget they were very tall, too," said Jacob. "They reared up on their hind legs. I'll bet they could eat the leaves on trees ten to twelve meters (30 to 35 ft) high."

"It's difficult to know exactly how tall they were," said Uncle Ned. "Certainly the *Brachiosaurus* could reach up to twelve meters (35 ft) so his shoulders would have been four meters (12 ft) above ground. *Barosaurus* could surely have reached three meters (9 ft) higher by rearing up on its hind legs. *Ultrasaurus* was taller, although no complete skeleton has been collected, and *Supersaurus* may have stood sixteen meters (52 ft)."

"I guess the smaller ones didn't weigh more than a few hundred grams (or ounces)," Jacob said, "but it says here that *Brachiosaurus* weighed over seventy-five tonnes (82 t) and *Ultrasaurus* up to eighty tonnes (88 t)."

"*Supersaurus* is estimated to have weighed approximately one hundred tonnes (110 t). Equal to a herd of fifteen African elephants." Uncle Ned laughed at everyone's surprise. "And he was about thirty-eight meters (125 ft) long. *Diplodocus* and *Apatasaurus* were long too — seven to eight meters (25 to 28 ft). They had long necks and whip-like tails with at least eighty vertebrae."

"Just as I said," pronounced Christine, "big monsters!"

"I don't think they would have been monsters, but they were big," said Father. "We will talk about them some more, but for now, let's all take a lunch break. It's my treat. Where do you want to go?"

"For hamburgers!" the children answered.

Allosaurus and *Brachiosaurus*
The massive *Brachiosaurus*, a giant among the herbivores, was 22.5 m (74 ft) long and weighed 77 tonnes (65 t)! It was 16.5 m (54 ft) when standing upright. Notice his nostrils in the top of his head. *Allosaurus*, a 12-m (39-ft) -long carnivore is especially small when compared with one of the giants of the North American dinosaurs. It was about 2 m (6.5 ft) at the hip. *Rhamphorhynchus*, a graceful pterosaur, flies high over the scenic tropical background.

Ornamentation

"Well, I guess we don't know exactly how dinosaurs looked when they were alive," Mother said. "We have their bones, of course, but do we know what was on those bones, Ned?"

"Good question, Mom," said Jacob who was returning to their table with more chips and a drink. "I've often wondered what color they were and if they were fat or sleek."

"There is some direct evidence and a few clues about their appearance. From this information, paleontologists have come to some conclusions. For example, we can tell from our observations of how muscles work on living animals plus our study of the dinosaur head shield that some dinosaurs were well equipped to fight and defend themselves. The *Triceratops* had a considerable area in the head shield for muscle attachment to support the head and give forceful drive to the horns when necessary. The horns were certainly useful but they probably served as ornamentation as well. They could have been used to attract females or scare off competition during mating season."

"Did males and females look alike?" Christine asked.

"Probably males had the most noticeable horns and probably the best coloring, too — like many animals today. Male birds are frequently more brightly colored and some male reptiles acquire bright colors during mating season. We suspect this would be true of dinosaurs as well," Uncle Ned replied.

Christine sounded disappointed and Uncle Ned had to admit that although each sex had its own distinguishing characteristics, it was usually males that were the biggest in size and had the best display of horns.

"If you consider hadrosaurs or the duck-billed dinosaurs, however, I can tell you that there were only slight differences in the head ornamentation between the sexes. The crests on the head may have acted as sound resonators to produce distinctive calls or they may have been used to bellow an alarm to warn off the approach of an enemy. The long tubular cavity filling these crests may have enhanced their sense of smell as well. The crests were certainly diversified and showed that this group had a variety of forms that continued right up to the time dinosaurs became extinct."

"It sure would be interesting to know how they fought each other and other animals," said Jacob.

"Well, the ankylosaurs were well equipped to protect themselves," continued Uncle Ned. "This group of dinosaurs had a general squat appearance so they could hug the ground, and they had a defensive armor of plates, many with protective spines to protect any exposed parts of the body. They had tail clubs, too, formed from bones embedded in the skin. The tail could act as a club and would have been a considerable threat to an enemy. These tail clubs are unique to ankylosaurs."

Ouranosaurus and *Spinosaurus*
Here are two dinosaurs that lived about 90 to 120 million years ago in Africa. Notice that both have large skin "sails" above their backs. *Spinosaurus* had sharp knife-like teeth, indicating that it was a meat eater and clearly a relative of *Tyrannosaurus*. The sails were thought to be heat exchangers, but quite likely served for recognition by others as well. One wonders what it was about the environment that would cause both *Spinosaurus* (12 m or 39 ft long), a carnivore, and *Ouranosaurus* (7 m or 23 ft long), a herbivore, to both develop a tall back fin.

Do We Know About Dinosaur Behavior?

"When an entire group of animals dies and leaves no living descendants, it's very difficult to know how they behaved when they lived on earth. Is there any way we would know what they did and how they did it?" Father directed his question to Uncle Ned.

"As always we look for clues," Uncle Ned began. "For example, some fossil remains have been found at the bottom of a preserved burrow so the animal must have spent part of its life underground. By the way the tail is constructed, we believe it could have been used for fighting and the horns could have been used for this purpose as well. We have casts of the brain cavities of dinosaurs and the size and complexity suggest the brains were larger than in comparably sized living reptiles — more like mammals. They had good hearing and sight so they were probably quite active with accompanying complex behavior."

"Were dinosaurs good parents?" asked Jacob.

"I think so," Uncle Ned said. "In the nests we've found in North America the embryos in the eggs have been at different stages of development. The juveniles were of different ages too, and were often still about the nest so this suggests that the parents were providing responsible care and were keeping out the egg-eating and carnivorous dinosaurs."

"Did dinosaurs hunt other animals?" asked Christine.

"Again, we think some did," said Uncle Ned. "Preserved trackways suggest that flesh-eating dinosaurs stalked their food. We also know that they were sociable animals and traveled in herds."

"Did males court females?" asked Jason.

"Dinosaurs probably had quite a complex courtship behavior," continued Uncle Ned. "The ceratopsions' horns may have been used as much for display to a female as for combat. Some modern reptiles have dewlaps or air sacs that are inflated to be attractive or to assist in their calling for mates. Dinosaurs probably did the same. Some head butting to undo the dominance of a competitor in courtship has been suggested for pachycephalosaurs, which was probably much the same as rams' behavior when they compete for a ewe's favor. So much about the animals is not known but it's surprising how much we learn from the clues we find in fossils."

"I'll say," said Jason. "I had no idea fossils were so valuable."

Maiasaurus

The name *Maiasaurus* means "good mother lizard" and is probably very descriptive of the dinosaur as a parent. The nests we have found are separated from each other by an adult body length (about 7 m or 23 ft) and are abundant in Montana. There is good evidence that they cared for their young after hatching. Notice the young in the illustration are hatched with soft feathers for insulation. As the baby grows larger, it will depend more on its own body heat and will have less need of feathers. Also notice the good mother bringing berries to the nest to feed the young.

What Did They Eat?

"Can anyone tell what dinosaurs ate?" Christine was very curious because Uncle Ned was talking about some dinosaurs that ate other animals and some that ate only plants.

"Their teeth certainly provide some definite answers about diet," Uncle Ned told her. "Look at this tooth, Christine. It's a simple elongated cone which was common to most carnivores."

"This one seems to have a little curve toward the back," said Jacob who was looking over Christine's shoulder.

"That would help the animal to hold his victim in a hook-like fashion," said Uncle Ned. "Some teeth are also serrated like a steak knife so the victim could be sliced up."

"If they don't have any flat chewing teeth they couldn't have chewed their food very well," said Christine.

"That's true," Uncle Ned replied. "If they were eating cycads or evergreens they would simply shred it to form a bolus for swallowing. For this shredding, they had rows of serrated teeth which scraped against one another in a way to be self-sharpening. As they wore out, they were replaced. Many dinosaurs lost teeth as well, and sometimes these have been found with the victim's remains. But the teeth seem to have grown again and this is true whether they were meat-eating theropods or plant-eating sauropods."

"But these ostrich-like ornithomimosaurs don't have any teeth at all," exclaimed Christine. "What did they eat?"

"These were probably the egg and insect eaters," said Jacob.

Uncle Ned agreed.

"If dinosaurs' teeth didn't chew the food, how did they digest it?" asked Jacob. "Were they like cows who have their food broken down by fermentation?"

"You may be right," said Uncle Ned. "In fact, that's a good idea. We also have record of gizzard or stomach stones found in many fossils. This suggests that the food went to the muscular gizzard where the tough vegetable fibres were ground finer for digestion. It certainly wasn't a unique situation. Some birds and alligators still do this today."

Apatasaurus and **Ornitholestes**

Apatasaurus (formerly called Brontosaurus) weighed over 30 tonnes (29 t) and was 21 m (69 ft) long! When standing on its back legs, as illustrated, it could reach about 9 m (30 ft) to feed on the leaves of trees.

Ornitholestes, a much smaller dinosaur, is equipped with a body for running. It has sharp teeth to catch small prey as illustrated.

Movement and Speed

"I know elephants are masters in the jungle simply because of their size," Jacob said. "So if I was a big heavy sauropod, I guess I wouldn't be too worried about other animals hunting me. But how could these big fossil bones move fast enough to escape the predators?"

"Well, don't forget they weren't just standard reptiles," Uncle Ned told him. "Dinosaurs could walk with erect limbs. They had progressed from their archeosaur ancestors to have more agile hips, knees, and ankles. That was the reason they could tuck their legs directly beneath their bodies to give them more stable support for their large size. This allowed them to be more efficient at running and walking."

"It's certainly an improvement over the waddling of alligators or turtles," Christine said. "But even so, I'm sure dinosaurs walked very slowly. Maybe they took big steps?"

"Well, we've studied some tracks we found in Texas and one of my colleagues in England developed a formula for computing the speed of dinosaurs. He related the toe-to-hip measurement with the length of the stride that was discovered by the footprints in the mud or sand. He said an average cruising speed was from three to six kilometers (1.8 to 3.6 mi) per hour. We think that a medium-sized predator on two limbs with a long stride could probably reach speeds of sixty-five kilometers (40 mi) per hour."

Christine was impressed. "I see that the bones of the two-legged dinosaurs are much more delicate so they would have been more agile. Do you think these creatures could have hopped about or were they just runners?"

Uncle Ned was very pleased with the children's interest. "Dinosaurs may have been able to balance themselves like kangaroos. Certainly they had a counter-balancing heavy tail for the heavy neck and trunk and legs in the front. This way they could probably move about very quickly without much thought of balance, and maybe they could hop or take big leaps."

"But even if some dinosaurs walked about on two legs and chased their prey, they probably came down on all fours to rest," said Jacob. "It would have been very tiring to keep that upright position all the time."

"Probably not," said Uncle Ned. "Ostriches and kangaroos either lie down or squat on their haunches to rest and dinosaurs may have done the same."

Dromiceiomimus

This dinosaur and its near relatives are known as the "ostrich dinosaurs" because of their resemblance to that bird. The dinosaur is found in western Canada and eastern Asia. With its large eyes and brain and slim proportions, it was undoubtedly a rapid and agile runner, as it is represented here running through a redwood forest. Probably its only means of defense was to escape. It has been calculated that it could run 30 km (19 mi) per hour. Its food was probably eggs and insects.

Weapons For Fighting

"Although vegetation-eating dinosaurs were usually gentle and probably minded their own business, that didn't keep them from being attacked by carnivorous or flesh-eating dinosaurs who wanted to eat them. These herbivores, as they were called, may not have been good fighters, but they were often protected by bony plates or spikes on their skin or else they had a large tail like the *Stegosaur* or three fierce horns like the *Triceratops*," noted Uncle Ned.

"But what about the carnivores," said Christine. "How did they attack?"

"Some saurischian dinosaurs, especially *Tyrannosaurus*, had such sharp, spike-like teeth that they could easily give a fatal bite," Uncle Ned told her. "And *Deinonychus*, one of several efficient hunting dinosaurs known as dromaeosaurids had a sickle-shaped claw on its inner back toes. It was probably covered by fingernail-like material like a cat's claw and with this slicing tool it could rip its victim to shreds like wolves attacking a caribou."

"Wow," Jacob exclaimed, "if a pack of those attacked an animal and caught it, it would be dead in a second."

"But look at these club tails," pointed out Christine. "You said this ankylosaurid was rather shy and retiring,

Uncle Ned, but one swing of that heavy bony tail would probably cripple an attacker. I think herbivores didn't need to fight."

"In some cases that was true," Uncle Ned replied. "Some herbivores by their sheer size were formidable opponents. Look at this stegosaurid. Not only does it have a huge heavy tail that it can lash about, but it has long sharp spikes on the tail as well. I'm sure it inflicted painful wounds and that would discourage a predator. In addition, some herbivores with fins, dewlaps, frills, or even a large heavy tail, could quite likely take several bites in these less critical areas without the bites being fatal. The frill on the ceratopsians would also deflect attacks and prevent punctures by the spines or horns of other dinosaurs."

"It might also trample it to death," laughed Jacob. "Look at the size of those feet!"

Euoplocephalus and *Albertosaurus*

These two dinosaurs, found in western Canada, were among the last dinosaurs before all dinosaurs became extinct. This illustration shows the armored ankylosaur using his massive tail for defense against the predator *Albertosaurus*. The tail club is an unusual defense amongst any animals. It could probably upset the carnivore, or perhaps even break its leg. *Albertosaurus* would find it difficult to get up if knocked down. Its front legs were nearly useless for this purpose because of their size.

Discovery

"I hope we find some fossil bones when we go with you to Alberta in the summer holidays, Uncle Ned," Christine said.

"It's probable that we will, although we won't be there very long," replied Uncle Ned. "We had more time when I went there with other paleontologists from Canada and China a few years ago."

"Was that expedition more important than the American Museum of Natural History expedition to the Gobi desert in the 1920s?" Jacob asked.

"When they contribute any good bone finds they're all important — even the finds of ranchers or farmers or tourists when they're out in their fields. They call us to come and see them and we're always very excited to locate something new. You can never tell how it will help us solve some of the mysteries of the past."

"What will happen if I find some bones?" asked Jacob.

"First we'll excavate all around them and then we'll wrap them in strips of burlap soaked in plaster of paris to make a field package. This way the bones are protected during their journey back to the museum. If the bone is fractured we may need to put some temporary hardener on it so it can be transported. If enough bones are found, sometimes we mount them in an exhibit so everyone can see them."

"But what if pieces are missing or the bones are all crushed," said Christine. "I know you make casts of them for exhibits but where do you store the real bones?"

"Right here," said Uncle Ned. "We always hope we'll find more so we can someday put the skeleton together."

"I love looking at these old bones and the rocks, too," said Jacob. "It's amazing to learn about dinosaurs from such clues. Will I be able to study the bones under a microscope?"

"Yes, of course. I plan to have everything set up for you."

"I know you refer to dinosaurs as reptiles, Uncle Ned, but some of them behave like birds and mammals. Their legs don't sprawl under their bodies and some even walk upright on two legs. They nest, take care of their young, and hunt in packs. It doesn't sound like the reptiles I know — a crocodile, for example," said Christine.

"Christine, you're going to be a scientist," said Uncle Ned. "Such curiosity. Would you believe that some scientists think dinosaurs might have had feathers or hair. Some may even have been warm-blooded. But birds and dinosaurs are closely related. After all, they both lay shelled eggs. The first recognized bird was *Archaeopteryx*, but it's hard to say if it was a 'good' specimen of a bird or simply a reptile with feathers, which it used to catch insects or to parachute to the ground from a tree. There's another intriguing possibility. What if birds are descended from dinosaurs and are now feathered dinosaurs still with us?"

"Oh, Uncle Ned," the children cried. "Stop teasing us."

"I'm really serious," said Uncle Ned. "Maybe dinosaurs aren't extinct at all."

Oviraptor

This very unusual dinosaur, 1.5 to 2 m (5 to 7 ft) long, has been given a name that means "egg thief." This suggests that the almost toothless dinosaur lived by eating eggs or was an unusual herbivore. We assume it had a horny sheath covering the jaws similar to a turtle, and had two teeth in its upper jaw. Very good fossil material has been found in Mongolia, but it has close relatives in North America. The head is similar to a modern bird called a cassowary, with a horn on top of the skull. This was probably for sexual display.

Extinction

"In a way, I'm sorry the big dinosaurs aren't still with us," said Christine. "Can you imagine. They've been gone for sixty-five million years!"

"I wonder what really made them disappear," mused Jacob.

"There were probably many contributing causes," said Uncle Ned. "Suppose they got some terrible disease comparable to hoof-and-mouth disease that cattle get. That would certainly run through the herd and spread until they were all dead. Or suppose they had no way to protect the eggs from predators and all the babies were killed before they hatched. That would also slowly cause their extinction."

"But some dinosaurs had live births and didn't hatch eggs," said Jacob, "so that theory seems weak."

"You're right," said Uncle Ned. "We do know that as the continents drifted, weather patterns changed and this caused the redistribution of the flora and fauna. Dinosaurs may have come into contact with new plants or animals and new diseases for which they had no resistance. As the weather became colder, they could have migrated and those who didn't move could have succumbed because of diet and climate conditions."

"How strange that these creatures should be so sensitive," remarked Jacob. "They could warm themselves from the sun. If the sun's rays were less direct and the daylight hours were less, I'm sure that would have caused a good deal of stress. Of course, we don't know if some had feathers or hair to help warm them."

"Yes," said Uncle Ned. "And don't forget that less sunlight means less vegetation. Probably the herbivores went first and then the carnivores. A modern theory suggests that a large comet or meteorite struck the earth and exploded, sending clouds of dust and steam into the air. This cloud would block the sun and cool the earth's climate. If the dinosaurs couldn't adapt to the new set of conditions, they would die and be replaced by mammals and birds and other groups of reptiles."

Uncle Ned continued, "Other scientists believe that there was a gradual extinction occurring over thousands, if not millions, of years and that the extinction sixty-five million years ago was only of the last few kinds which were being replaced by more adaptable animals. I certainly favor this theory."

"That is a fascinating story," said Christine. "I wonder if we'll ever know exactly what happened."

Pachycephalosaurus

In the last few years of the dinosaur we notice the comet that will cause an explosion that is widely accepted to have spelled their doom. *Quetzalcoatlus*, a flying reptile, seems to be doing a fly-by to bid goodbye to this interesting group of animals. *Quetzalcoatlus* was the largest and last of the pterosaurs. The pachycephalosaurs surely used their domed heads for head butting in courtship combat. The higher domed one on the right is the male.

Field Work Bound

A few weeks later, when school was out, Uncle Ned made good his commitment to take Christine and Jacob to hunt for dinosaur fossils. They were to meet Uncle Ned at Red Deer, Alberta, and their parents were to drive them. First, however, they planned to visit some other well known fossil sites on the way.

The car trip was long and Christine and Jacob were restless. As they approached the badlands of South Dakota Jacob became more interested. "Look at the weird way the land is shaped," he said excitedly. "It looks like haystacks with colored bands through them."

"Yes," his father agreed. "This area is a lot like the badlands of the Red Deer Valley in Alberta. But of course these sites are only half as old as the ones we will work in with Uncle Ned. These badlands in South Dakota were laid down after the dinosaurs became extinct."

"You mean these sites are quite new," Jacob asked? "They look old to me."

Mother laughed, "Remember, Jacob, Uncle Ned told us the dinosaurs became extinct about sixty-five million years ago and the pamphlet on these badlands tells us they are only about thirty-three million years old. Time's ceaseless weathering has formed these beautiful hills in half the time."

They visited a local museum in Rapid City showing many of the large mammals that had been collected within the badlands of South Dakota. At the university museum the children learned that some mammals they thought were limited to other continents had a good portion of their evolution in North America. For example, camels existed here for millions of years before a branch of them went to South America to be guanacos, alpacas, and vicunas, and these later went to Asia and Africa to be the one- and two-humped camels we know today. Zebras, asses, horses, rhinoceroses, tapirs, and primates all had a long history on this continent. Before they became extinct here they provided stock for the examples that showed up later on other continents.

"That's interesting," Christine said. "These exhibits are filled with local fossils and they're all so big. Look at these titanotheres. They must have been descended from dinosaurs."

"I don't think so," Mother said. "It says here that the titanotheres are mammals whose ancestors arose from reptiles. They would have existed one hundred and fifty million years ago, so they were living at the same time as the dinosaurs. Dinosaurs are certainly reptiles, but like mammals they are descended from ancestral reptiles."

"Could you please hurry," Jacob called? He was impatient with all the exhibits. "I want to get on that dig with Uncle Ned."

Avimimus

It looks like a bird and that is what its name implies — bird mimic. It was found in deposits 70 to 90 million years old in Mongolia. It is quite possible that it had feathers along its "arms" which would make it an excellent runner to pursue insects, perhaps snaring them in its feathered net. Actual imprints of the feather attachment are on the arm bones, similar to a chicken. Its skeleton is quite bird-like as well. *Avimimus* existed just before the extinction of all dinosaurs.

Westward Bound

"We're all anxious to get to Alberta," Dad told them as they got back into the car, but Mother and I have planned another surprise. Since we are all interested in dinosaurs we plan to take a short detour to Dinosaur National Monument on the northern border between Utah and Colorado."

"Oh no! More museums," protested Jacob. "I want to dig up fossils, not look at mounted dinosaurs."

"Well, then, I'm sure you'll be surprised with this display," Mother replied.

The steeply dipping beds of the Jurassic formation, called the Morrison, represent sands and shales that had accumulated in a large river valley flowing from highlands in the south in New Mexico. It is this formation that forms a dramatic backdrop for the visitor center. Throughout the range of this formation dinosaurs have been collected for over a hundred years.

As they approached the visitor center, Jacob looked around in amazement.

"Wow," he exclaimed, "the fossil skeletons are actually in the rock and the paleontologists are working on them!" The people were dressed in yellow lab coats and hard hats as they removed the overburden with jackhammers and then did the finer collecting with small picks and brushes.

"I wonder why the fossils show up in near vertical walls," said Christine.

Dad explained. "The skeletal remains accumulated in the backwater of some ancient stream. Much later, when the skeletons hardened into shale and sandstone, the rock was folded into large wave-like forms, and when it was exposed, the fossils were collected from one of these near vertical folds."

"Look, Dad," called Jacob. "There are two clams next to the dinosaur's foot. So, they must have been preserved together."

Mother read from a label and said aloud. "Even the shale they remove is to be examined for creatures that may have lived there such as snails, crawdads, fish, and even the teeth of mammals."

Jacob looked puzzled. "Gosh, Christine. Remember the shelled animals that we picked up on our trip to the coast. I wonder why the dinosaurs are found with sea life?"

"These are freshwater snails and clams," Mother explained. "However, extensive sediments from this time and the later period were deposited beneath the sea. A great variety of fish, other shellfish, coral, and a variety of birds and swimming reptiles have been found in these marine sediments. This pamphlet says the reptiles were called ichthyosaurs, plesiosaurs, and mosasaurs. I'm sure there was a great variety of life living on land and in the water at the same time."

"Wow, what a place," exclaimed Jacob. "I'm glad we did stop here. But now let's go to see Uncle Ned."

Centrosaurus

In the past, centrosaurs migrated long distances similar to the way bison once traveled in large herds. Here, a herd is made up of some young, middle-aged, and older animals entering a swollen river. This story has been pieced together from a bone bed in Alberta, Canada. The centrosaur bones show evidence of being trampled and being chewed by carnivores, before they were finally buried, to be preserved in river sediments.

With Uncle Ned in Alberta

Finally Jacob and Christine and their parents joined Uncle Ned in Dinosaur Provincial Park about one hundred kilometers (62 mi) southeast of the well known Tyrrell Museum at Drumheller, Alberta. They met at the field station of the Tyrrell Museum where several people were helping Uncle Ned get ready to go on a "dig." A "dig" is the term paleontologists use to describe the site where they collect fossils.

"Well, are you ready to collect a dinosaur?" Uncle Ned asked. "We'll be collecting only a short distance from here where the Red Deer River has exposed two partial skeletons and hopefully a third complete one of the duck-billed dinosaurs. The rock is called the Judith River or Oldman formation and represents sands and muds that preserved the dinosaur bones about seventy-eight million years ago."

While Uncle Ned continued to prepare for the collecting, the children examined the field station.

"Come here, Christine," Jacob called. "You can see them preparing the fossils from field packages. I can hardly wait until tomorrow when we can help Uncle Ned."

The next day, two excited children and their parents joined Uncle Ned and his crew at the site.

"The sun is as hot as it was in the badlands in South Dakota," Christine observed. "There's no shade anywhere."

"This is a good place to collect fossil bones," Uncle Ned answered. "Because there are no trees the streams erode the banks very quickly and that way the bones are exposed."

While in the field they also looked for trace fossils and other geological clues. Uncle Ned explained that trace fossils are biological clues to the site. Tracks the animals had made, coprolites which are fossil excrement, "gizzard stones" which are the grinding stones used for digestion, and skin imprints in the mud provide indications of past life. "When you see mud cracks, that indicates the drying out of a water body. Ripple marks indicate waves formed by wind or moving water. Here are raindrop prints in this layer of shale."

The children were amazed, and Christine in particular, examined all the evidence very thoroughly. Jason, as usual, was anxious to get on to something new.

While Uncle Ned took notes on his map, the crew was hardening the exposed bones and making plaster jackets about the bones for protection in order to transport them back to the museum for further preparation and study.

After several days, Christine was still complaining about the heat and her sunburned nose. "It's hard work in the field, Uncle Ned, but I wouldn't trade this holiday for anything!"

Lambeosaurus

A male (the one with the larger crest) and a female are preparing for their annual migration to the south where there will be more abundant foods. The ginko trees are dropping their yellow leaves preparing for the long arctic night. A dusting of snow is noticed here and there on the ground. The sun at its highest is still low near the horizon. The two duckbills will probably join others for the long trek to southern latitudes.

After The Dig

After several days of working in the warm Alberta sun, the children went with Uncle Ned to see that their field packages were secured in the field station. The packages were well marked as to locations so the site could be revisited if necessary. The data also included the date and the collector's name.

"Good documentation of where the collections were made and who collected them is very important," Uncle Ned explained. "This way the specimens can be related to field notes and observations made during the collection."

Later that evening Uncle Ned joined the family in their hotel for dinner. The children were still bubbling with excitement and had questions about the dinosaurs' behavior, intelligence, and size. As Uncle Ned answered one question another one arose.

"I guess mammals are smarter than reptiles," Jacob began, "but how intelligent were dinosaurs?"

"A dinosaur called *Stenonychosaurus* was found right here in Alberta and it is considered the 'brainiest' of them all," Uncle Ned answered. "The brain cavity is the largest proportional to its body size, about two meters (6.5 ft) long. Its brain would be about the size of an emu's so it would be about as intelligent as an opossum, which is one of the least intelligent of living mammals."

Christine was fascinated. "Is that how you tell?" she asked, "by size?"

"These kinds of comparisons can be risky," Uncle Ned agreed. "Personally I like to consider other anatomical features as well. Some dinosaurs seem to possess large eyes and a well-developed brain. This, along with their light build and the shape of their limbs, suggests that they might well be agile sprinters with good reflexes and well-developed senses. They were probably good at catching insects. Probably good at night hunting, as well, and hunting in packs such as wolves do now."

Christine was delighted with Uncle Ned's information. "Perhaps there are hints about their intelligence from their behavior," she said. "You did mention that paleontologists know how they fed and fought."

"Yes, that's true," Uncle Ned answered. "Now and then new clues are discovered that explain the probable behavior of dinosaurs. Recently tracks were found in Virginia where a carnivore track showed that the hunter used considerable stealth to creep up on potential food. The prints show that he stopped in his tracks, without moving his feet, then continued on by rocking back on his heels to pursue his prey again. He probably stopped to assess his situation — you know, listen, smell, and observe — before he continued. If we observed this happening, we would say it shows intelligence. He was planning ahead. Other trackways illustrate predators following their prey doggedly and this takes intelligence too. Other tracks show that herds of dinosaurs traveled together, with the adults on the outside and younger ones in the center, probably for protection."

"Oh, Uncle Ned," Christine said. "I think you have the most interesting job in the world!"

Stenonychosaurus
This 2 m (6.5 ft) bird-like dinosaur is found in Alberta and is referred to as *Troodon* in some books. It had better binocular vision than any other dinosaur and likely hunted at night. The feathers on the back are speculation, but probably occurred on several dinosaurs. Flowering plants are becoming more common and notice the small tree-climbing mammal (called *Alphadon*) in the magnolia tree. This dinosaur is considered to be one of the smartest, having the brain size of *Alphadon*, a distant relative of the opossum.

Departure

The next morning during breakfast, the children still had many questions. Christine announced that she was going to become a paleontologist and Uncle Ned said that she could help in the Museum on Saturdays.

"I'm anxious to see what you will do with the egg fragments we found the other day," Christine said. "Uncle Ned, do you think most dinosaurs were hatched from eggs?"

"It's hard to say," Uncle Ned replied. "Some modern reptiles such as snakes give birth to live young. And there has been an ichthyosaur found with young still preserved within the mother's body as well as a couple of newly born beside the mother. The mother probably died while giving birth. Because of these examples, I think it would be fair to assume that at least some dinosaurs gave live birth. There is also another line of evidence. Some of the large sauropod dinosaurs have very large birth canals, large enough to accommodate about a quarter of the adult size. This suggests the capacity to give birth to a rather large baby, maybe up to a hundred kilograms (220 lbs)! It's reasonable to suppose that such a large dinosaur would need to start out its life fairly large. Some dinosaurs were probably warm-blooded, like mammals, which supports this theory too. It's interesting that no eggs have ever been found of the larger dinosaurs."

"Uncle Ned," Jacob interrupted, "did dinosaurs sit on the eggs to hatch them, like chickens do?"

"Probably not," reckoned Uncle Ned. "My guess is that the eggs would not support the parents. More likely the eggs were hatched by the heat generated by decaying vegetation brought to the nest by the parents, similar to the way alligators hatch their young. Or maybe they were like turtles where hatching depends on the radiated heat from the sun."

Dad was listening to this conversation and decided to ask a question of his own. "Ned, there has been some discussion in popular science magazines about small dinosaurs, no bigger than a chicken, as well as embryos being found in eggs along with youngsters about the nest. How do they know all small dinosaurs are not just young ones that would have eventually grown up?"

"That's a good question," answered Uncle Ned, "and paleontologists are not in complete agreement about this. Generally you can tell age by the degree of cementation at the ends of growing bones. Many of the young fossils associated with nest sites here in Alberta and in Montana are definitely young because the growing surfaces on the bones show that they have considerable growth to add. Other cases are not as clear. An interesting study done several years ago, comparing the stage of development of a group of ornithopods with the domestic turkey, did show that the ornithopods were adult. Hatchling ostriches and chickens were compared as well. Again it was determined that the ornithopods were adults although only about the size of a chicken. It's interesting, but there has been very little study of this kind."

Christine and Jacob thought they would like to help unravel some of these mysteries. After the past several months, they knew that dinosaurs would always be a subject of interest to them.

Compsognathus and *Archeopteryx*
The illustration of two theropods, one with feathers and one without, shows the probable transition from reptile to bird. *Compsognathus* shows a few feathers. Were it not for the preserved feathers of *Archeopteryx* the latter would have been the same reptile. The skeletons of the two are so similar that one would be mistaken for the other. Here *Compsognathus* (the size of a chicken) chases *Archeopteryx* (the size of a crow). It is suspected *Archeopteryx* dined on fish because of the shape of its teeth and claws which are similar to living fish eaters. The pterosaurs (flying reptiles) probably competed for a short time with the first birds.